TRAINS of

UPPER MIDWEST

PHOTO ARCHIVE

Steam and Diesel in the 1950s & 1960s

Marvin Nielsen

Iconografix
Photo Archive Series

Iconografix, Inc.
PO Box 446
Hudson, Wisconsin 54016 USA

Library of Congress Card Number: 00-135950

ISBN 1-58388-036-4

01 02 03 04 05 06 07 5 4 3 2 1

Printed in the United States of America

Cover and book design by Shawn Glidden

Copy editing by Dylan Frautschi

Cover Photo: Milwaukee Road E-9 33A and FP-7 103C are at New Lisbon, Wisconsin, with trains 58 and the Afternoon Hiawatha No. 2. No. 58 left Minneapolis three hours earlier than No. 2 but did much local business, so No. 2 caught up and passed it at New Lisbon. New Lisbon was the location of the CMStP&P branch line to Wausau and Tomahawk, Wisconsin.

Book Proposals

Iconografix is a publishing company specializing in books for transportation enthusiasts. We publish in a number of different areas, including Automobiles, Auto Racing, Buses, Construction Equipment, Emergency Equipment, Farming Equipment, Railroads & Trucks. The Iconografix imprint is constantly growing and expanding into new subject areas.

Authors, editors, and knowledgeable enthusiasts in the field of transportation history are invited to contact the Editorial Department at Iconografix, Inc., PO Box 446, Hudson, WI 54016.

Noon train. One of the author's favorite photos is this one of Omaha train No. 80 at the Sioux Falls, South Dakota, station. The photo typifies a station stop of a day local train. The car men are checking equipment on coach 750, the milk cans have been unloaded and the mail and express are being loaded. Soon, at 11:50 a.m. the conductor will give a highball and 4-6-2 385 and its train will be off across the prairie.

INTRODUCTION

This book is an album of photos taken by the author in Wisconsin, Minnesota, and South Dakota. The photos were taken during the 1950s and 1960s when the change from steam to diesel power was being made. Represented are freight and passenger trains of the following railroads:

Train riding for me started at a young age. As a kindergartner in 1938 I rode with the rest of the class on Northern Pacific train 51 from Central Avenue station in Superior to the downtown Superior Union station. I also remember riding Northern Pacific No. 52 once or twice from Duluth to Central Avenue after a shopping trip with my mother.

My first real train trip took place in the summer of 1946 when my mother and I went from Superior to Sioux Falls, South Dakota, to visit a sister and her family that lived there. When I think about it now, it was amazing the places one could go on the train back then, even though it may have involved riding on several trains and railroads to get to your destination.

Our trip in 1946 began at 4:45 p.m. on Great Northern train No. 19, "the Gopher," to Minneapolis. At Minneapolis we had a couple hour wait at Great Northern station for CStPM&O train No. 209, "the Mondamin." There were many rail travelers then and I can remember the coach we were on being pretty well filled. We were lucky to be able to have facing walk over seats that night. We were in an open window coach so I recall riding with my head out the window most of the night watching the steam engine. After a 186 mile, seven hour trip (209 was an all stops train with much head end business) we arrived in Worthington, Minnesota, at 5:20 a.m. Train No. 83, the local passenger train to Sioux Falls, was waiting on the station siding. Coach passengers had to change trains. There was a through Minneapolis-Sioux Falls sleeper that was switched from No. 209 onto No. 83. At 5:25, we were off onto the branch-line to Sioux Falls. We also rode in an open window coach on No. 83, so after 62 miles of watching 4-6-2 383 operate out of an open window, I had a face full of coal dust and cinders. The trip back to Superior was a reversal of the procedure via CStPM&O 82 and 210 and on Great Northern No. 24 from St. Paul to Superior.

I made this trip each year for several years. On one trip Great Northern No. 19 was headed by a 4-6-2 (1355 possibly) which was the only time I ever had a chance to ride behind Great Northern steam. On one other trip going back to Superior the CStPM&O was late arriving in St. Paul so we were put on the Northern Pacific No. 62 to Duluth. No. 62 did not serve Superior, but entered Duluth via the Carlton-Duluth short line. I can remember what a great sight it was from the train, dropping downhill into Duluth.

On one trip that I kept notes on, the following equipment was used. This was from Sept. 3, 1950. Omaha No. 82 out of Sioux Falls at 10:50 p.m. had 4-6-2 383 on the head end with coach 750. CStPM&O 210 was headed by 4-6-2 511 out of Worthington with coach 6105. Great Northern No. 24 had 267 for power and coach 964. One thing that impressed me on that trip was waking up early from sleeping on the coach seat and being able to hear the 511 racing at full throttle along the Minnesota River bottoms with our train. After Omaha 82 and 83 were discontinued it was still possible to make connections to Sioux Falls via the Great Northern. The trip then involved taking Great Northern No. 19 from Superior to Minneapolis, Great Northern No. 9, "The Dakotan," to Willmar, and Great Northern No. 51 to Sioux Falls, arriving at 8:30 a.m. The schedules on the return trip on the GN were not very convenient so an auto ride was in order from Sioux Falls to Worthington to catch the C&NW North American to Minneapolis to make a connection with N.P. No. 66 to Superior. No. 66 on that trip was pulled by 4-6-2 No. 2246. A stop at Central Ave. station at 5:29 a.m. was made for me to detrain.

Before we were married I talked my wife-to-be into riding the caboose on the Soo Line mixed train on the Ridgeland line from Barron to Ridgeland and return. Needless to say this was a strange new event for her. We were pulled by 2-8-0 472 that day and rode the cupola on caboose 170.

In the 1960s, I introduced my kids to riding the rails by driving to Cambridge, Minnesota, and taking Great Northern No. 24 to Duluth and spending the afternoon there and then riding the parlor car on No. 19 back to Cambridge in the early evening. I operated a business for several years and always tried to use passenger train service whenever I could on business trips.

When I was very young my sister taught school at Rhinelander, Wisconsin. When she would come home to Superior to visit she would have to ride the train. She would take the C&NW from Rhinelander to Ashland and connect there with Northern Pacific 51 for Superior. This train, usually a B series gas-electric, went right by our house. I can remember playing outside one day and No. 51 stopped at our back yard. They had stopped the gas-electric there to drop off my sister instead of at the station a one-half mile away. What great service.

When I was in high school I had a couple buddies that I chummed with pretty regularly. On some Saturday nights we would head for downtown Superior to a movie or a dance usually taking the city bus or hitch hiking. Occasionally, on the way home we would ride Northern Pacific No. 65 (from Superior to Central Avenue). This activity seemed to irritate the agent at the Union station to no end. Since his shift ended when 65 left at 12:06 a.m. and the depot was closed he was not at all pleased to sell three 15¢ tickets to Central Avenue. He used to tell us to go ride the city bus, which we refused to do. He finally got wise and told us to buy our tickets from the conductor, who didn't at all object to us riding.

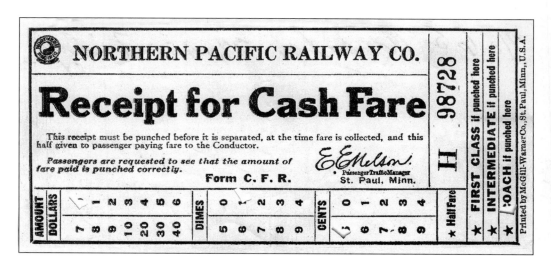

One of the most fascinating things about a steam locomotive was its whistle. One could identify which railroad the engine was operating on by the sound of the whistle and each locomotive whistle had a distinct tone of its own. Even though there was a prescribed set of whistle signals one could sometimes tell which engineer was operating the locomotive by the way he delivered the whistle signal. The most common signal used was for a road crossing which were two long blasts, one short and one long. This was the signal where an engineer could show his own style; varying the length of the long blasts, giving just a short toot for the short and perhaps easing off on the whistle cord on the last blast to end softly.

I can remember being in bed as a youngster with the windows open on a hot summer night. Even though our house was more than one-half mile from Northern Pacific Central Avenue station, one could hear the engineer on No. 65, the midnight train to Minneapolis, whistle one long blast to announce his approach to the station and to let the Great Northern tower operator know that No. 65 needed a clear signal to cross the Great Northern tracks. He would then whistle for 58th Street and then for 61st Street. After a short station stop the train would move away from the station, cross the Great Northern, and then one could hear the loud rumble in the still of the night air as the train crossed the long wood piling bridge across the Pokegema River. A whistle signal would be sounded for the Cemetery road crossing and the sound of No. 65 would fade off into the distance. Often shortly after No. 65 had passed, a freight would follow. The lead engine would pass the station and proceed across the Pokegema River with its train. The helper engine would be cut off on the fly from the caboose and stop at the water plug for water. After the fireman filled the tender with water one could hear him bang shut the cover on the tender. Still having a green signal, the helper would cross the Great Northern, proceed slowly across the Pokegema River bridge and couple up to the train. After coupling was completed, the helper engineer would sound two long blasts on the whistle to let the head end engineer know they were ready to roll. The engineer on the head end would answer with two long blasts. The lead engine would start the train, so by the time the slack ran out to the rear of the train the helper engine would take off like a rabbit.

Most people wonder why anyone would be so interested in trains, particularly real trains (usual comment upon the mention of railroads "Oh yes, my cousin George has a model railroad in his basement"). Once a person became familiar with the operation of a railroad, it was and still is a fascinating hobby. Several of the photos in the book were taken at Sioux Falls, South Dakota. This might not seem to be a very likely place for train action, but in the 1950s the city was served by five railroads, the CStPM&O, the CRI&P, the Illinois Central, the Great Northern, and the Milwaukee Road. Each railroad had its own depot and interestingly enough in the year 2000, four of them are still standing. The only one demolished was the Omaha's.

I would like to thank my wife Eleanor for her work typing and to thank my grandson Tony for his work on the computer to help me with this book.

CStPM&O Mikado 404 hurries along with a southbound freight about three miles south of Sarona, Wisconsin. This part of the Omaha's Superior-Eau Claire main line has been abandoned.

Omaha J class 2-8-2 No. 404 passes the station at Rice Lake, Wisconsin, with a way freight on November 25, 1955.

Omaha 2-8-2 404 has delivered a car of coal to the local creamery at Cameron, Wisconsin, and is returning to its train with an empty hopper car. Lines of the CStPM&O and the Soo Line crossed at Cameron. The photo shows the control tower for the crossing and the depots of the Omaha and Soo. An old hotel is pictured at the left.

CStPM&O 2-8-2 404 sits on the siding at Cameron, Wisconsin, with its train, as 2-8-2 419 storms past with a northbound freight.

CStPM&O 2-8-2 413 takes the siding while Mikado 440 holds the mainline as their trains meet at Bloomer, Wisconsin, on March 3, 1956.

CStPM&O E class Pacific 508 departs the station at Duluth, Minnesota, with train No. 512, the "Arrowhead Limited," for Chicago. This station was also used by the DW&P Railway Trains.

Omaha 4-6-0 361 leaves the Spooner, Wisconsin, station with mixed train No. 244-245 for Park Falls, Wisconsin. This train departed Spooner on Mon.-Wed.-Fri. and returned from Park Falls as train 246-243 on Tues.-Thurs.-Sat.

CStPM&O class I-1 4-6-0 361 is southbound near Haugen, Wisconsin, with train No. 244, the mixed train for Park Falls, Wisconsin. Note combine car on the rear of the train.

Omaha 4-6-0 357 is at the Cumberland, Wisconsin, station with a mixed train, No. 68, operating from Spooner to Hudson, Wisconsin.

Omaha I-1 4-6-0s 357 and 361 are at the Spooner, Wisconsin, roundhouse after bringing in trains from Hudson and Park Falls, Wisconsin.

C&NW F7 unit 4071-C is at Green Bay, Wisconsin, with train No. 216, the "Flambeau 400," for Chicago, Illinois. Equipment on this train included parlor, lounge, and a dining car.

Omaha 4-6-0 322 is at the yard office in Sioux Falls, South Dakota. 322 was used for switching and also for helper duty on westbound freights. Pullman "Chippewa" in the foreground is part of the equipment that came in as part of train No. 83 at 7:40 a.m. and will lay over for the day at Sioux Falls and depart as train No. 82 at 10:50 p.m. Great Northern station is in the background.

Omaha Road 4-6-0 245 and 4-6-2 383 double-head a freight from Mitchell, South Dakota, entering the yard at Sioux Falls, South Dakota. The passenger equipment is part of trains 82 and 83 that had a lay over at Sioux Falls during the day. Photo taken on September 7, 1949.

CStPM&O 4-6-0 224 heads Mitchell, South Dakota-Worthington, Minnesota, train No. 80 on August 30, 1950. The train will arrive shortly in Sioux Falls, South Dakota, at 11:30 a.m. The photographer climbed one of the few willow trees on the South Dakota prairie to photograph the train.

CStPM&O I-2 class Pacific type 383 has brought train No. 83 into Sioux Falls, South Dakota, from Worthington, Minnesota, at 7:40 a.m. on July 24, 1950. No. 83 had much head-end business and carried a through-Pullman from Minneapolis received from Omaha train No. 209 at Worthington.

C&NW motor car 2002 with Omaha train No. 80 from Mitchell, South Dakota, crosses Duluth Avenue in Sioux Falls, South Dakota, on July 24, 1950. This train will continue on to Worthington, Minnesota, to make a connection at 2:30 p.m. with CStPM&O train No. 204 for Minneapolis.

It's 4:00 p.m. on July 23, 1951 at Worthington, Minnesota, and CStPM&O train 203, "The North American," has just arrived from Minneapolis with E8 unit 5010 on the head end. 4-6-2 383 stands on the adjacent track with train No. 81 for Sioux Falls and Mitchell, South Dakota.

Omaha class M-3 0-6-0 No. 86 switches the yard at Sioux Falls, South Dakota, on July 31, 1950.

4-6-0 235 is at the roundhouse at Sioux Falls, South Dakota.

E8 unit 5018 heads the C&NW flagship Chicago-Minneapolis train, "The 400," at the station at Eau Claire, Wisconsin.

Menu

Commuter Streamliners Leaving
North Western Station, Chicago,
During Evening Rush Hour.

Chicago and Northwestern train No. 400 is just west of Eau Claire, Wisconsin, where it will stop at 1:53 p.m. on its run from Minneapolis to Chicago.

Five Chicago and Northwestern GP7s are parked at Rice Lake, Wisconsin, while the crew has lunch.

In June of 1956, class M-3 2-8-8-4 No. 229 heads a train of iron ore out of Hibbing, Minnesota, on the Duluth, Missabe and Iron Range line to Hull Jct., on its way to the yards at Proctor, Minnesota.

DM&IR Yellowstone type 2-8-8-4 223 is at Adolph, Minnesota, with a train of iron ore for the yards at Proctor, Minnesota.

Duluth, Missabe & Iron Range 2-8-8-4 No. 228 passes through Iron Jct., Minnesota, on its way to Proctor, Minnesota, with a trainload of iron ore from the east range. DM&IR lines from the east and west ends of the Mesabi iron range converged at Iron Jct. Date is Oct. 16, 1955.

Duluth, Missabe & Iron Range 228 stands on the wye track at the Mitchell, Minnesota, engine house. Eighteen 2-8-8-4s Nos. 220-237 were built for the DM&IR by Baldwin Locomotive Works in 1941 and 1943.

DM&IR 2-10-4 Texas Types 700 and 705 are at the engine house at Mitchell, MN, on April 18, 1956.

DM&IR 2-8-8-4 No. 221 drifts downgrade just north of Two Harbors, Minnesota, with a train of iron ore for the yards at Two Harbors. The track at the left is used by trains of empty cars from the Two Harbors yard returning to the Iron Range for loading.

DM&IR 2-8-8-4 No. 231 passes the scene of a wreck at the yards in Biwabik, Minnesota. Date is June 30, 1956.

Duluth, Missabe, and Iron Range 2-8-0 1204 switches cars at the local freight house at Hibbing, Minnesota, on August 8, 1956.

A superstitious engineer might turn down a call to run the 1313 for the day. Here DM&IR 2-8-2 1313 is shown at 3rd Avenue West in Hibbing, Minnesota.

Duluth, Missabe & Iron Range M-2 2-8-8-2 No. 210 heads for work at Hibbing, Minnesota, on April 28, 1956. These engines were used for transferring cars of iron ore from the mine loading facilities to a marshalling yard for shipment to Proctor, Minnesota.

On Sept. 14, 1955, DM&IR (ex-B&LE) 2-10-4 713 heads a transfer run of iron ore at Hibbing, Minnesota.

Duluth, Missabe & Iron Range 2-10-2 514 heads a railfan extra train for Virginia, Minnesota. The train is at the Duluth, Minnesota, station on Sept. 2, 1962.

With business car "Northland" on the rear end, DM&IR Pacific type No. 400 heads a passenger extra to Duluth, Minnesota, at Wilpen, Minnesota.

DM&IR SD-9s lug a train of empty ore cars up the hill from the docks at Duluth to the yard at Proctor, Minnesota. White structures in the background are an oil pipeline tank farm at Superior, Wisconsin.

Occasionally during the change from steam to diesel power the Duluth, Missabe, & Iron Range borrowed locomotives from its sister road, the Bessemer and Lake Erie. Here an A-B-B set of Bessemer F units, with 725 in the lead, is shown near Wilpen, Minnesota, in April of 1956.

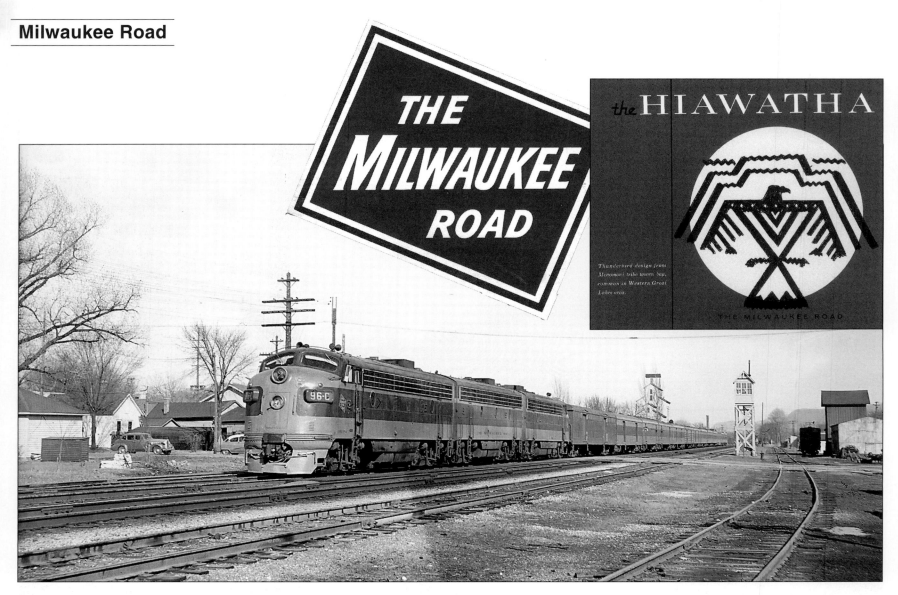

FP7 96C with Milwaukee Road No. 6, the "Morning Hiawatha," to Chicago, approaches the station at Winona, Minnesota.

Milwaukee Road Morning Hiawatha departs Minneapolis, Minnesota, on a cold winter day.

It is 4:00 p.m. and the engineer on FP7 unit 91A looks back for a highball from the conductor to depart the Sioux Falls, South Dakota, station for Chicago with Milwaukee Road train, the "Arrow." This train will join the section of the Arrow operating out of Omaha, Nebraska, at Manilla, Iowa, for the overnight trip into Chicago.

ALCO RSC2 979 heads train No. 22, the Sioux, at the station in Sioux Falls, South Dakota. No. 22 will depart at 3:35 p.m. for its journey across northern Iowa, southern Wisconsin, and northern Illinois, to Chicago.

Milwaukee Road 4-6-2 817 heads Chicago-bound train, the Arrow, upgrade out of the Sioux River valley just out of Sioux Falls, South Dakota, on Sept. 3, 1950.

Taken at the same location as the photo on the previous page, steam power no longer rules and E-7 17B now provides power for the Arrow.

E-7 17B crosses the Big Sioux River just a short distance from Sioux Falls, South Dakota, station with the Midwest Hiawatha to Chicago.

Milwaukee Road F5 4-6-2 825 is the power for No. 22, the Sioux, at Sioux Falls, South Dakota, on July 23, 1950.

Milwaukee Road engineer oils around Mikado 564 on the ready track at the Sioux Falls, South Dakota, engine house on July 19, 1950.

CMStP&P class L2 2-8-2 491 crosses the Big Sioux River with a mainline freight for the yard at Sioux Falls, South Dakota, on July 21, 1950.

F3 units 81 A and B stand on the ready track at the Milwaukee Road Sioux Falls, South Dakota, engine house.

Milwaukee Road 4-6-0 1062 backs to the Sioux Falls, South Dakota, roundhouse after bringing in a local freight from the north.

Milwaukee Road C2 2-8-0 1321 stands outside the Sioux Falls, South Dakota, roundhouse on July 19, 1950.

Out in the middle of the southwestern Minnesota farm country the Austin, Minnesota, to Madison, South Dakota, line of the Milwaukee Road crossed the Minneapolis-Omaha line of the CStPM&O. Located about 15 miles north of Worthington, Minnesota, the crossing was called Miloma (Milwaukee & Omaha) and consisted of an impressive station but not much else. Shown here is a Milwaukee Road 2-8-0 1247 at Miloma with No. 203, the daily except Sunday mixed train.

Great Northern train No. 162 has arrived at the Sioux Falls, South Dakota, station from Yankton, South Dakota, with motor car 2328. After loading mail, express, and passengers, the train will leave for an 18 mile run to Garretson, South Dakota, where it will make a connection with Great Northern train No. 52 for Willmar, Minnesota.

Great Northern motor car 2317 is ready to leave the station at Sioux Falls, South Dakota, with train No. 54, the daily except Sunday local to Watertown, South Dakota.

Great Northern 4-6-2 1436 is at the Great Northern engine house in north Sioux Falls, South Dakota. GN 1436 is an H-3 class Pacific built in 1907 by Baldwin.

Great Northern H-4 Pacific type 1458 backs past the depot, heading for the roundhouse, at Sioux Falls, South Dakota, after bringing in a train on July 27, 1950.

Great Northern H-3 Pacific type 1412 waits with a circus train to enter the yard at Sioux Falls, South Dakota. The train is off the Watertown, South Dakota, line and is stopped on the bridge over the Big Sioux River. Photo taken on July 27, 1950.

Great Northern Baldwin P-2 4-8-2 2523 is at Willmar, Minnesota.

Heavy 0-7 class Mikado 3383 is in storage at the Great Northern roundhouse at Willmar, Minnesota.

Great Northern GP-7 635 has picked up three empty cattle cars from the John Morrell plant at Sioux Falls, South Dakota. The railroads serving Sioux Falls all shared in the traffic from this large packing plant.

A freight with three units, including GP35s 3021 and 3012, passes the train entrance to the Minneapolis passenger station. The train approaching is Great Northern No. 8, the Winnipeg Limited.

Ex-Great Northern (B.N.) GP-7 1355 (GN 906) does some switching at Minneapolis.

Great Northern U25B 2521 and a heater car are at the Great Northern engine facilities at Union Station in St. Paul, Minnesota. 2521 was not equipped with train heating equipment so it was necessary to attach a car with a boiler to provide heat for the cars in a passenger train.

Great Northern train No. 19, the Gopher, with E-7 512 is at the Duluth, Minnesota, Union Station. It will soon depart on its 160-mile run to Minneapolis-St. Paul, with stops at Superior, Wisconsin, and Sandstone and Cambridge, Minnesota.

E-7 502 heads Great Northern No. 24, the "Badger," past the small station at Dedham, Minnesota, 14 miles from Superior. Burlington Northern abandoned this stretch of track for a route into Superior over the ex-Soo Line.

Great Northern E-7 503 heads the "Gopher," train No. 19, out of Superior, Wisconsin, on its fast 2 1/2-hour run to Minneapolis.

If schedules were being kept, Grandy, Minnesota, was the place that Great Northern train Nos. 23 & 24 met each day. No. 24 to Duluth is shown in the siding while No. 23 to Minneapolis passes on the main line.

An A-B-A lash-up of Great Northern F units is at 61st Street in Superior heading for the yards at Allouez.

This photo and those on the following two pages show a meet between Soo Line Duluth-Minneapolis train Nos. 62 and 63 at Frederic, Wisconsin. Above photo shows GP-9 551 heading into the siding after finishing its work at the Frederic, Wisconsin, station.

No. 551 has entered the siding and waits as Soo Line No. 62 with FP7 unit 505 passes on the main line.

The meet with No. 62 being completed, No. 63 moves back onto the main line to complete its run to Minneapolis-St. Paul. Note the conductor on the rear platform inspecting No. 62 as it passed. This line from near Dresser, Wisconsin, to MJ tower just out of Superior, Wisconsin, has been abandoned.

Class H-23 Pacific 2718 roars past the Soo Line depot at Deronda, Wisconsin. Train is a Minnesota railfan extra bound for Barron, Wisconsin, and a trip down the branch line to Ridgeland, Wisconsin, on August 12, 1956.

Soo Line 2718 crosses Hwy. 25 at Hillsdale, Wisconsin, with a railfan special. Hillsdale once had pickle vats railside where cucumbers were stored until they could be shipped via Soo Line to a pickle factory in Minneapolis.

Soo Line GP-9 558 switches the small yard at Rice Lake, Wisconsin.

Soo Line GP-7 378 prepares to leave the station at Rice Lake, Wisconsin, after delivering cars of coal and logs to various industries in town.

F3 unit 201B passes through Cameron, Wisconsin, with a Soo Line freight for Shoreham yard in Minneapolis, Minnesota.

East bound Soo Line freight with F7 unit 2203 passes the station at Colfax, Wisconsin.

Soo Line 2-8-0 472 switches the grain elevator at Dallas, Wisconsin, in October 1954. Photo was taken from the cupola of caboose 170. Train No. 71 was a mixed train that ran on the 19-mile Barron-Ridgeland branch.

The Soo Line station at Dallas, Wisconsin, was typical of many stations on the Soo. Dallas was located on a 19-mile branch line from Barron to Ridgeland, Wisconsin.

NOTICE TO THE PUBLIC

Abandonment between Barron and Ridgeland, Wisconsin

Pursuant to Order of the Interstate Commerce Commission dated September 24, 1962, in Finance Docket 21675 authorizing abandonment of the line of railroad between Barron and Ridgeland, Wisconsin, Soo Line Railroad Company hereby gives notice to all concerned as follows:

Effective 12:01 A.M. Thursday, November 15, 1962, Soo Line Railroad Company will abandon its branch line of railroad extending southward from a point near Barron in Barron County, Wisconsin, at Railroad Milepost 90 plus 423 feet, Station 23 plus 00 to the end of the track at Ridgeland in Dunn County, Wisconsin.

The last train scheduled under existing timetables and service will be operated on Monday, November 12, 1962, and the stations of Dallas, Hillsdale and Ridgeland will close permanently as of the close of business on November 14, 1962.

Attention is directed to applicable tariff supplement attached hereto.

Dated October 31, 1962.

SOO LINE RAILROAD COMPANY

By _T. R. Klingel_
T. R. Klingel, Vice President -
Operating and Maintenance

Soo Line crews take up the rails near Highway A just north of Ridgeland, Wisconsin, in 1963. A copy of the abandon order for the Barron-Ridgeland Line is shown.

Class H-20 Pacific 2700 crosses the Nemadji River about 10 miles south of Superior with train No. 63 for Minneapolis on a winter day in 1953. This bridge is now used by the BNSF for its route to Superior.

Soo Line 2-8-0s 2449 and 2438 are parked at the yard in Ashland, Wisconsin, serving out their last years in ore steaming service. Cars in background are part of the equipment for train No. 118 leaving at 5:55 p.m. for Chicago.

The Soo Line lettered switcher 2119 "SUPERIOR" in honor of a celebration of railroad days in Superior, Wisconsin.

Northern Pacific W-3 2-8-2 1833 passes the Central Avenue, Superior, Wisconsin, station with a transfer run to East End, Superior, on March 3, 1957.

Baldwin-built class Q-3 4-6-2 No. 2164 pauses on May 15, 1950 at Central Avenue station, Superior, Wisconsin, with Northern Pacific train No. 55 for Staples, Minnesota. No. 55 provided connections at Staples with the "North Coast Limited" for points west to Seattle.

Mikado W-3 type 1807 serves as a helper out of Superior on an extra freight headed by 2-8-2 1841 on the Northern Pacific. Train is at Cemetery Road crossing just after crossing the Pokegema River on the trestle in the background.

Northern Pacific 2-6-2 Prairie type 2467 works the yard at East End, Superior, Wisconsin.

4-8-4 2686 has been turned at Staples, Minnesota, and will couple up to the cars of a Minnesota Railfan Special to return to Minneapolis. RDC at station is equipment for train No. 56 to Duluth.

Northern Pacific U25C 2527 with a sister engine 2526 and a geep are power for freight out of Northtown yard in Minneapolis.

Northern Pacific GP-7 232 rides the turntable at the Northern Pacific Northtown roundhouse in Minneapolis.

Northern Pacific F7 unit 6511A heads train No. 1, the "Mainstreeter," into Minneapolis. The train is crossing the Mississippi River just prior to entering Union Station.

Northern Pacific F7 unit 6508C arrives at Union Station, Minneapolis, from Seattle with No. 26, the "North Coast Limited."

Northern Pacific W-3 class 2-8-2 1791 heads a transfer run of iron ore to the Great Northern at Allouez yard in Superior, Wisconsin. 2-8-2 1805 serves as a helper, on this very cold winter day in November 1956. The Northern Pacific ore dock is shown behind 1791 and the Great Northern ore docks are shown behind 1805.

CB&Q E unit 9966 slows for a stop at Winona Jct., Wisconsin, with N.P. train, the Mainstreeter. The Chicago to Seattle trains of the Northern Pacific and Great Northern used the Burlington route between Chicago and St. Paul.

CB&Q 9988 stops at Altoona, Wisconsin, for a crew change. Floods on the Mississippi River in April of 1965 forced the CB&Q to re-route Minneapolis to Chicago trains over the C&NW. Train shown is the combined North Coast Limited-Empire Builder.

Four Burlington units headed by GP-30 941 are at the St. Paul, Minnesota, engine house.

CB&Q A-B-A F3 units are at the St. Paul, Minnesota, servicing area.

CB&Q A-B-B F3 units with cab unit 136-D are at St. Paul, Minnesota.

CB&Q 4-8-4 5632 pauses for a photo run with a railfan extra at Nelson, Wisconsin.

CB&Q class S-4 4-6-4 3003 leaves Alma, Wisconsin, with a railfan extra in September 1957.

Rock Island BL-2 425 is at the Sioux Falls, South Dakota, engine house. The engine house, turntable, and the yards are now gone without a trace and have been replaced by housing and other municipal developments.

Rock Island BL-2 427 switches the yard at Sioux Falls, South Dakota. Water tank in background was still used to service an occasional 2-8-0 or 4-6-2.

4-6-2 833 has just brought Rock Island train No. 19 into Sioux Falls, South Dakota, at 11:10 a.m. and is being turned on the turntable. It will be serviced in preparation for heading train No. 20 leaving at 12:30 p.m. No. 833 was built in 1905 and was one of the older Pacifics on the CRI&P.

The engineer on Rock Island motor car 9010 checks for a highball from the conductor and will leave the station at Sioux Falls, South Dakota, with train No. 20 at 12:30 p.m. This train operated across Iowa and was an all stops local to Cedar Rapids, Iowa. The date is September 7, 1949.

Rock Island GP7 1203 has picked up a car from the Illinois Central in a switch move at Sioux Falls, South Dakota. The engine is crossing the Big Sioux River on a bridge that was later destroyed in a flood.

Rock Island Alco freight-hauler 143 is at the Inver Grove engine house in St. Paul, Minnesota.

Two F7 units with 101 in the lead prepare to take a freight out of the Rock Island yards at St. Paul.

Rock Island E8 unit 653 is at the Milwaukee Road station in Minneapolis with train No. 17, "The Plainsman," for Kansas City. The Plainsman was remnant of the Twin Star Rocket, which once traveled over 1300 miles to Houston, Texas.

THE PLAINSMAN

Dinner

Tomato Juice .40   Fresh Orange Juice .40
Chicken Noodle Soup .40

Filet of Sole, Tartar Sauce.. 2.10
One-Half Fried Chicken, Southern Style.. 2.50
Roast Sirloin of Beef 2.75

Scalloped Potates   Green Beans
Hearts of Lettuce, French Dressing
Cloverleaf Rolls
Freshly Baked Pie   Jello with Whipped Cream
Chocolate Sundae
Coffee   Tea   Milk

SALADS
Chef's Salad Bowl, Julienne of Ham and Cheese, Hard Boiled Egg...... 1.25
California Fruit Plate, Cottage Cheese, Raisin Bread............................. 1.00

HOT SELECTIONS
Old Fashioned Beef Stew with Garden Fresh Vegetables, Rolls............ 1.45
Open-Faced Corned Beef Sandwich on Rye Bread, Dill Pickle.............. 1.20
Chili Con Carne with Saltines.. .80
Jumbo Hamburger on Sesame Bun, Pickle, Sliced Onion, Potato Chips.. 1.05

COLD SANDWICHES
Baked Sugar Cured Ham... .95
Sliced Turkey 1.05
Cheddar Cheese.. .75
Ham and Cheese... .85
(Served with Pickle and Potato Chips)

DESSERTS
Jello with Whipped Cream.. .35
Freshly Baked Pie.. .45
Vanilla Ice Cream with Cookies.. .40
Chocolate Sundae .... .45

Half portions served at half price to children under 12 years of age.
Please write each item desired on Meal Check.
Waiters are forbidden to serve orders GIVEN ORALLY.
J. S. Antink, Manager—Food Services, Rock Island Lines, Chicago, Ill.

17-18   E-1-G 750

Rock Island E-7 unit 637 heads train No. 17, "The Plainsman," for Kansas City in Minneapolis. This train carried coaches and a diner.

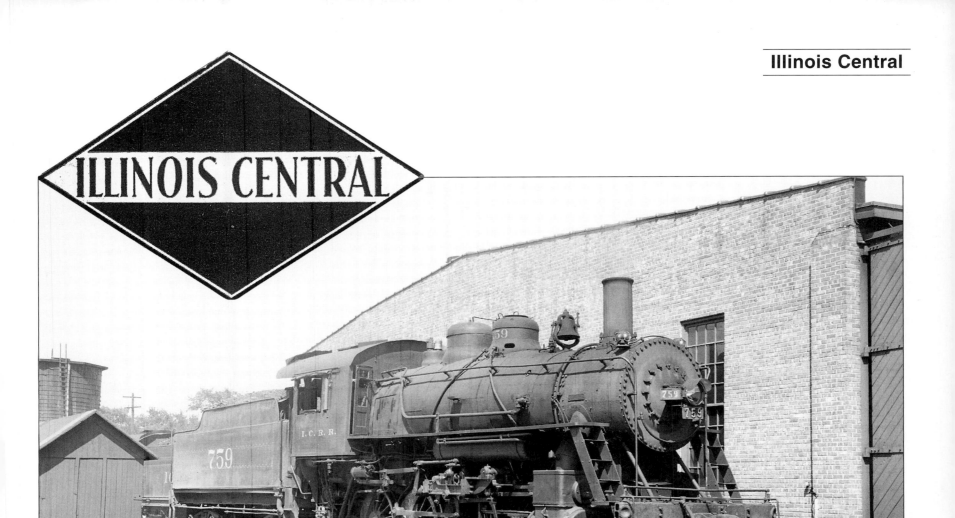

2-8-0 759 is at the Illinois Central engine house at Sioux Falls, South Dakota, on a hot summer day in 1950. 759 is a snappy-looking, light consolidation type.

Illinois Central Pacific 1001 arrives at the I.C. Sioux Falls, South Dakota, station at 11:30 a.m. on July 31, 1950 with mixed train No. 741 from Cherokee, Iowa. A coach for passengers is the first car behind the engine.

Illinois Central 4-6-2 1002 leaves Sioux Falls, South Dakota, with a local freight for Cherokee, Iowa. The Illinois Central line out of Sioux Falls has been abandoned.

Illinois Central geep 8951 takes several cars away from the stock pens at the John Morrell meat packing plant at Sioux Falls, South Dakota.

Alco road switcher 304 waits work assignment at the Norwood yard in Green Bay.

Green Bay and Western Alco units 302 and 311 are at the GB&W engine facilities in Green Bay, Wisconsin.

Green Bay and Western Alco unit 311 is at the engine house and shops at Green Bay.

Green Bay and Western Alco switcher 102 rides the turntable at Green Bay.

Chicago Great Western cow and calf switcher 66 is at State Street yard in St. Paul.

Passenger F unit 152 heads Chicago Great Western train No. 14 from Omaha into the station in Minneapolis. Nos. 13 and 14 were the last scheduled passenger trains on the CGW.

Canadian National class J-4 4-6-2 No. 5133 brings DW&P train No. 20 from Ft. Francis, Ontario, across the wood piling bridge that was the approach to the station at Virginia, Minnesota. It's 6:50 a.m. and after a station stop No. 20 will be off on the last 77 miles of its run to Duluth.

Some of the iron ore mining companies on the Mesabi iron range operated their own railroad systems to haul iron ore to the surface of the open pit mines, to be loaded on G.N. or DM&IR trains. Two of the Hoyt Mining Co. 0-6-0s, 75 and 78, are pictured working at Hibbing, Minnesota, in December 1955.

MORE TITLES FROM ICONOGRAFIX:

AMERICAN CULTURE

AMERICAN SERVICE STATIONS 1935-1943 PHOTO ARCHIVE .... ISBN 1-882256-27-1
COCA-COLA: A HISTORY IN PHOTOGRAPHS 1930-1969 .... ISBN 1-882256-46-8
COCA-COLA: ITS VEHICLES IN PHOTOGRAPHS 1930-1969 .... ISBN 1-882256-47-6
PHILLIPS 66 1945-1954 PHOTO ARCHIVE .... ISBN 1-882256-42-5

AUTOMOTIVE

CADILLAC 1948-1964 PHOTO ALBUM .... ISBN 1-882256-83-2
CAMARO 1967-2000 PHOTO ARCHIVE .... ISBN 1-58388-032-1
CORVETTE THE EXOTIC EXPERIMENTAL CARS, LUDVIGSEN LIBRARY SERIES .... ISBN 1-58388-017-8
CORVETTE PROTOTYPES & SHOW CARS PHOTO ALBUM .... ISBN 1-882256-77-8
EARLY FORD V-8S 1932-1942 PHOTO ALBUM .... ISBN 1-882256-97-2
IMPERIAL 1955-1963 PHOTO ARCHIVE .... ISBN 1-882256-22-0
IMPERIAL 1964-1968 PHOTO ARCHIVE .... ISBN 1-882256-23-9
LINCOLN MOTOR CARS 1920-1942 PHOTO ARCHIVE .... ISBN 1-882256-57-3
LINCOLN MOTOR CARS 1946-1960 PHOTO ARCHIVE .... ISBN 1-882256-58-1
PACKARD MOTOR CARS 1935-1942 PHOTO ARCHIVE .... ISBN 1-882256-44-1
PACKARD MOTOR CARS 1946-1958 PHOTO ARCHIVE .... ISBN 1-882256-45-X
PONTIAC DREAM CARS, SHOW CARS & PROTOTYPES 1928-1998 PHOTO ALBUM .... ISBN 1-882256-93-X
PONTIAC FIREBIRD TRANS-AM 1969-1999 PHOTO ALBUM .... ISBN 1-882256-95-6
PONTIAC FIREBIRD 1967-2000 PHOTO HISTORY .... ISBN 1-58388-028-3
STUDEBAKER 1933-1942 PHOTO ARCHIVE .... ISBN 1-882256-24-7
ULTIMATE CORVETTE TRIVIA CHALLENGE .... ISBN 1-58388-035-6

BUSES

BUSES OF MOTOR COACH INDUSTRIES 1932-2000 PHOTO ARCHIVE .... ISBN 1-58388-039-9
THE GENERAL MOTORS NEW LOOK BUS PHOTO ARCHIVE .... ISBN 1-58388-007-0
GREYHOUND BUSES 1914-2000 PHOTO ARCHIVE .... ISBN 1-58388-027-5
MACK® BUSES 1900-1960 PHOTO ARCHIVE* .... ISBN 1-58388-020-8
TRAILWAYS BUSES 1936-2001 PHOTO ARCHIVE .... ISBN 1-58388-029-1

EMERGENCY VEHICLES

AMERICAN LAFRANCE 700 SERIES 1945-1952 PHOTO ARCHIVE .... ISBN 1-882256-90-5
AMERICAN LAFRANCE 700 SERIES 1945-1952 PHOTO ARCHIVE VOLUME 2 .... ISBN 1-58388-025-9
AMERICAN LAFRANCE 700 & 800 SERIES 1953-1958 PHOTO ARCHIVE .... ISBN 1-882256-91-3
AMERICAN LAFRANCE 900 SERIES 1958-1964 PHOTO ARCHIVE .... ISBN 1-58388-002-X
CLASSIC AMERICAN AMBULANCES 1900-1979 PHOTO ARCHIVE .... ISBN 1-882256-94-8
CLASSIC AMERICAN FUNERAL VEHICLES 1900-1980 PHOTO ARCHIVE .... ISBN 1-58388-016-X
CLASSIC AMERICAN LIMOUSINES 1955-2000 PHOTO ARCHIVE .... ISBN 1-58388-041-0
CLASSIC SEAGRAVE 1935-1951 PHOTO ARCHIVE .... ISBN 1-58388-034-8
FIRE CHIEF CARS 1900-1997 PHOTO ALBUM .... ISBN 1-882256-87-5
LOS ANGELES CITY FIRE APPARATUS 1953 - 1999 PHOTO ARCHIVE .... ISBN 1-58388-012-7
MACK MODEL C FIRE TRUCKS 1957-1967 PHOTO ARCHIVE* .... ISBN 1-58388-014-3
MACK MODEL CF FIRE TRUCKS 1967-1981 PHOTO ARCHIVE* .... ISBN 1-882256-63-8
MACK MODEL L FIRE TRUCKS 1940-1954 PHOTO ARCHIVE* .... ISBN 1-882256-86-7
NAVY & MARINE CORPS FIRE APPARATUS 1836 -2000 PHOTO GALLERY .... ISBN 1-58388-031-3
PIERCE ARROW FIRE APPARATUS 1979-1998 PHOTO ARCHIVE .... ISBN 1-58388-023-2
POLICE CARS: RESTORING, COLLECTING & SHOWING AMERICA'S FINEST SEDANS ISBN 1-58388-046-1
SEAGRAVE 70TH ANNIVERSARY SERIES PHOTO ARCHIVE .... ISBN 1-58388-001-1
VOLUNTEER & RURAL FIRE APPARATUS PHOTO GALLERY .... ISBN 1-58388-005-4
WARD LAFRANCE FIRE TRUCKS 1918-1978 PHOTO ARCHIVE .... ISBN 1-58388-013-5
YOUNG FIRE EQUIPMENT 1932-1991 PHOTO ARCHIVE .... ISBN 1-58388-015-1

RACING

GT40 PHOTO ARCHIVE .... ISBN 1-882256-64-6
INDY CARS OF THE 1950s, LUDVIGSEN LIBRARY SERIES .... ISBN 1-58388-018-6
INDIANAPOLIS RACING CARS OF FRANK KURTIS 1941-1963 PHOTO ARCHIVE .... ISBN 1-58388-026-7
JUAN MANUEL FANGIO WORLD CHAMPION DRIVER SERIES PHOTO ALBUM .... ISBN 1-58388-008-9
LE MANS 1950: THE BRIGGS CUNNINGHAM CAMPAIGN PHOTO ARCHIVE .... ISBN 1-882256-21-2
MARIO ANDRETTI WORLD CHAMPION DRIVER SERIES PHOTO ALBUM .... ISBN 1-58388-009-7
NOVI V-8 INDY CARS 1941-1965 KARL LUDVIGSEN LIBRARY SERIES .... ISBN 1-58388-037-2
SEBRING 12-HOUR RACE 1970 PHOTO ARCHIVE .... ISBN 1-882256-20-4
VANDERBILT CUP RACE 1936 & 1937 PHOTO ARCHIVE .... ISBN 1-882256-66-2

RAILWAYS

CHICAGO, ST. PAUL, MINNEAPOLIS & OMAHA RAILWAY 1880-1940 PHOTO ARCHIVE ISBN 1-882256-67-0
CHICAGO & NORTH WESTERN RAILWAY 1975-1995 PHOTO ARCHIVE .... ISBN 1-882256-76-X
GREAT NORTHERN RAILWAY 1945-1970 PHOTO ARCHIVE .... ISBN 1-882256-56-5
GREAT NORTHERN RAILWAY 1945-1970 VOL 2 PHOTO ARCHIVE .... ISBN 1-882256-79-4
MILWAUKEE ROAD 1850-1960 PHOTO ARCHIVE .... ISBN 1-882256-61-1
MILWAUKEE ROAD DEPOTS 1856-1954 PHOTO ARCHIVE .... ISBN 1-58388-040-2
SHOW TRAINS OF THE 20TH CENTURY .... ISBN 1-58388-030-5
SOO LINE 1975-1992 PHOTO ARCHIVE .... ISBN 1-882256-68-9

TRAINS OF THE TWIN PORTS, DULUTH-SUPERIOR IN THE 1950s PHOTO ARCHIVE .. ISBN 1-58388-003-8
TRAINS OF THE CIRCUS 1872-1956 PHOTO ARCHIVE .... ISBN 1-58388-024-0
TRAINS OF THE UPPER MIDWEST: STEAM & DIESEL IN THE 1950S & 1960S .... ISBN 1-58388-036-4
WISCONSIN CENTRAL LIMITED 1987-1996 PHOTO ARCHIVE .... ISBN 1-882256-75-1
WISCONSIN CENTRAL RAILWAY 1871-1909 PHOTO ARCHIVE .... ISBN 1-882256-78-6

TRUCKS

BEVERAGE TRUCKS 1910-1975 PHOTO ARCHIVE .... ISBN 1-882256-60-3
BROCKWAY TRUCKS 1948-1961 PHOTO ARCHIVE* .... ISBN 1-882256-55-7
CHEVROLET EL CAMINO PHOTO HISTORY INCL GMC SPRINT & CABALLERO .... ISBN 1-58388-044-5
DODGE PICKUPS 1939-1978 PHOTO ALBUM .... ISBN 1-882256-82-4
DODGE POWER WAGONS 1940-1980 PHOTO ARCHIVE .... ISBN 1-882256-89-1
DODGE POWER WAGON PHOTO HISTORY .... ISBN 1-58388-019-4
DODGE TRUCKS 1929-1947 PHOTO ARCHIVE .... ISBN 1-882256-36-0
DODGE TRUCKS 1948-1960 PHOTO ARCHIVE .... ISBN 1-882256-37-9
FORD HEAVY DUTY TRUCKS 1948-1998 PHOTO H STORY .... ISBN 1-58388-043-7
HEAVY RESCUE TRUCKS 1931-2000 PHOTO GALLERY .... ISBN 1-58388-045-3
JEEP 1941-2000 PHOTO ARCHIVE .... ISBN 1-58388-021-6
JEEP PROTOTYPES & CONCEPT VEHICLES PHOTO ARCHIVE .... ISBN 1-58388-033-X
LOGGING TRUCKS 1915-1970 PHOTO ARCHIVE .... ISBN 1-882256-59-X
MACK MODEL AB PHOTO ARCHIVE* .... ISBN 1-882256-18-2
MACK AP SUPER-DUTY TRUCKS 1926-1938 PHOTO ARCHIVE* .... ISBN 1-882256-54-9
MACK MODEL B 1953-1966 VOL 1 PHOTO ARCHIVE* .... ISBN 1-882256-19-0
MACK MODEL B 1953-1966 VOL 2 PHOTO ARCHIVE* .... ISBN 1-882256-34-4
MACK EB-EC-ED-EE-EF-EG-DE 1936-1951 PHOTO ARCHIVE* .... ISBN 1-882256-29-8
MACK EH-EJ-EM-EQ-ER-ES 1936-1950 PHOTO ARCHIVE* .... ISBN 1-882256-39-5
MACK FC-FCSW-NW 1936-1947 PHOTO ARCHIVE* .... ISBN 1-882256-28-X
MACK FG-FH-FJ-FK-FN-FP-FT-FW 1937-1950 PHOTO ARCHIVE* .... ISBN 1-882256-35-2
MACK LF-LH-LJ-LM-LT 1940-1956 PHOTO ARCHIVE* .... ISBN 1-882256-38-7
MACK TRUCKS PHOTO GALLERY* .... ISBN 1-882256-88-3
NEW CAR CARRIERS 1910-1998 PHOTO ALBUM .... ISBN 1-882256-98-0
PLYMOUTH COMMERCIAL VEHICLES PHOTO ARCHIVE .... ISBN 1-58388-004-6
REFUSE & RECYCLING TRUCKS PHOTO ARCHIVE .... ISBN 1-58388-042-9
STUDEBAKER TRUCKS 1927-1940 PHOTO ARCHIVE .... ISBN 1-882256-40-9
STUDEBAKER TRUCKS 1941-1964 PHOTO ARCHIVE .... ISBN 1-882256-41-7
WHITE TRUCKS 1900-1937 PHOTO ARCHIVE .... ISBN 1-882256-80-8

TRACTORS & CONSTRUCTION EQUIPMENT

CASE TRACTORS 1912-1959 PHOTO ARCHIVE .... ISBN 1-882256-32-8
CATERPILLAR PHOTO GALLERY .... ISBN 1-58388-070-0
CATERPILLAR POCKET GUIDE THE TRACK-TYPE TRACTORS 1925-1957 .... ISBN 1-58388-022-4
CATERPILLAR D-2 & R-2 PHOTO ARCHIVE .... ISBN 1-882256-99-9
CATERPILLAR D-8 1933-1974 INCLUDING DIESEL 75 & RD-8 PHOTO ARCHIVE .... ISBN 1-882256-96-4
CATERPILLAR MILITARY TRACTORS VOLUME 1 PHOTO ARCHIVE .... ISBN 1-882256-16-6
CATERPILLAR MILITARY TRACTORS VOLUME 2 PHOTO ARCHIVE .... ISBN 1-882256-17-4
CATERPILLAR SIXTY PHOTO ARCHIVE .... ISBN 1-882256-05-0
CATERPILLAR TEN INCLUDING 7C FIFTEEN & HIGH FIFTEEN PHOTO ARCHIVE .... ISBN 1-58388-011-9
CATERPILLAR THIRTY 2ND ED. INC. BEST THIRTY, 6G THIRTY & R-4 PHOTO ARCHIVE ISBN 1-58388-006-2
CLETRAC AND OLIVER CRAWLERS PHOTO ARCHIVE .... ISBN 1-882256-43-3
CLASSIC AMERICAN STEAMROLLERS 1871-1935 PHOTO ARCHIVE .... ISBN 1-58388-038-0
FARMALL CUB PHOTO ARCHIVE .... ISBN 1-882256-71-9
FARMALL F– SERIES PHOTO ARCHIVE .... ISBN 1-882256-02-6
FARMALL MODEL H PHOTO ARCHIVE .... ISBN 1-882256-03-4
FARMALL MODEL M PHOTO ARCHIVE .... ISBN 1-882256-15-8
FARMALL REGULAR PHOTO ARCHIVE .... ISBN 1-882256-14-X
FARMALL SUPER SERIES PHOTO ARCHIVE .... ISBN 1-882256-49-2
FORDSON 1917-1928 PHOTO ARCHIVE .... ISBN 1-882256-33-6
HART-PARR PHOTO ARCHIVE .... ISBN 1-882256-08-5
HOLT TRACTORS PHOTO ARCHIVE .... ISBN 1-882256-10-7
INTERNATIONAL TRACTRACTOR PHOTO ARCHIVE .... ISBN 1-882256-48-4
INTERNATIONAL TD CRAWLERS 1933-1962 PHOTO ARCHIVE .... ISBN 1-882256-72-7
JOHN DEERE MODEL A PHOTO ARCHIVE .... ISBN 1-882256-12-3
JOHN DEERE MODEL B PHOTO ARCHIVE .... ISBN 1-882256-01-8
JOHN DEERE MODEL D PHOTO ARCHIVE .... ISBN 1-882256-00-X
JOHN DEERE 30 SERIES PHOTO ARCHIVE .... ISBN 1-882256-13-1
MINNEAPOLIS-MOLINE U-SERIES PHOTO ARCHIVE .... ISBN 1-882256-07-7
OLIVER TRACTORS PHOTO ARCHIVE .... ISBN 1-882256-09-3
RUSSELL GRADERS PHOTO ARCHIVE .... ISBN 1-882256-11-5
TWIN CITY TRACTOR PHOTO ARCHIVE .... ISBN 1-882256-06-9

*This product is sold under license from Mack Trucks, Inc. Mack is a registered Trademark of Mack Trucks, Inc. All rights reserved.

All Iconografix books are available from direct mail specialty book dealers and bookstores worldwide, or can be ordered from the publisher. For book trade and distribution information or to add your name to our mailing list and receive a **FREE CATALOG** contact:

Iconografix, PO Box 446, Hudson, Wisconsin, 54016   Telephone: (715) 381-9755, (800) 289-3504 (USA), Fax: (715) 381-9756

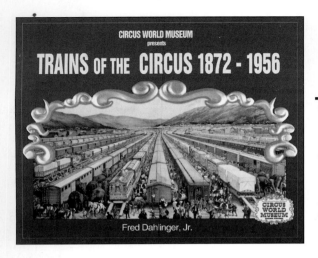

TRAINS OF THE CIRCUS 1872 - 1956

Fred Dahlinger, Jr.

MORE GREAT BOOKS FROM ICONOGRAFIX

TRAINS OF THE CIRCUS 1872-1956 PHOTO ARCHIVE
ISBN 1-58388-024-0

SHOW TRAINS OF THE 20TH CENTURY
ISBN 1-58388-030-5

MILWAUKEE ROAD DEPOTS 1856-1954 PHOTO ARCHIVE
ISBN 1-58388-040-2

MILWAUKEE ROAD 1850-1960 PHOTO ARCHIVE
ISBN 1-882256-61-1

WISCONSIN CENTRAL LIMITED 1987-1996 PHOTO ARCHIVE
ISBN 1-882256-75-1

GREYHOUND BUSES 1914-2000 PHOTO ARCHIVE
ISBN 1-58388-027-5

TRAINS OF THE TWIN PORTS, DULUTH-SUPERIOR IN THE 1950s PHOTO ARCHIVE
ISBN 1-58388-003-8

ICONOGRAFIX, INC. P.O. BOX 446, DEPT BK, HUDSON, WI 54016
FOR A FREE CATALOG CALL:
1-800-289-3504

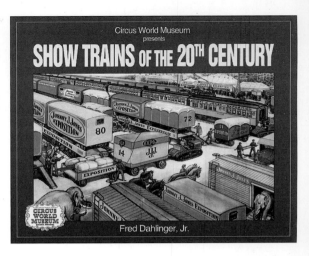

Circus World Museum presents

SHOW TRAINS OF THE 20TH CENTURY

Fred Dahlinger, Jr.

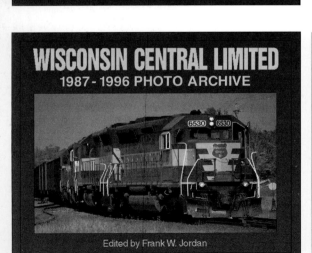

MILWAUKEE ROAD DEPOTS
1856 - 1954 PHOTO ARCHIVE

Kim D. Tschudy

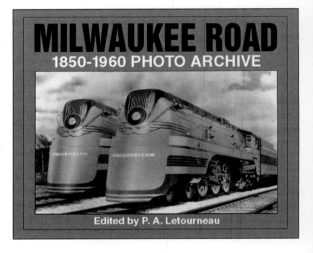

MILWAUKEE ROAD
1850-1960 PHOTO ARCHIVE

Edited by P. A. Letourneau

WISCONSIN CENTRAL LIMITED
1987 - 1996 PHOTO ARCHIVE

Edited by Frank W. Jordan

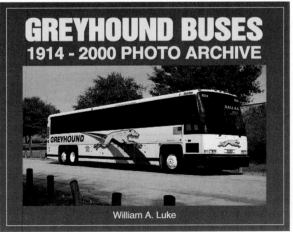

GREYHOUND BUSES
1914 - 2000 PHOTO ARCHIVE

William A. Luke

TRAINS OF THE TWIN PORTS
PHOTO ARCHIVE
DULUTH-SUPERIOR in the 1950s

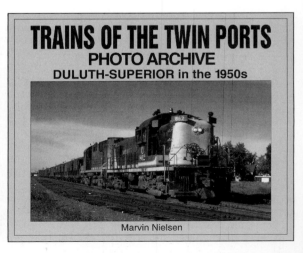

Marvin Nielsen